His Word Came By Grace

Susan Leffler

Written and illustrated by Susan Leffler, but inspired by the Holy Spirit.

Hi. My name is Grace, but everyone calls me Gracie.
This is my puppy Oscar. I want to tell you
about the Word of God.

God created the heavens and the earth by His spoken word.
When God said, "Let there be light," there was light.
Then He spoke forth the sun and the moon and water
and land and birds and animals and plants
and all the creatures of the sea... everything!

All were created by the spoken word of God!

Then God said, "Let there be light"; and there was light.
Genesis 1:3

By the word of the Lord the heavens were made, and all the host of them
by the breath of His mouth.
Psalm 33:6

God sent His Word in the form of a man,
and that man was Jesus, the Son of God.

Jesus gave us grace, which is favor from God,
and truth, which is in the word of God.

Jesus taught the people many things when
He was here on the earth. But you know what?
He still teaches us by His word in the bible.

In the beginning was the Word and the Word was with God, and the Word was God.
John 1:1-2

And the Word became flesh and dwelt among us, and we beheld
His glory as of the only begotten of the Father, full of grace and truth.
John 1:14

And you shall know the truth, and the truth shall make you free.
John 8:32

For the law was given through Moses, but grace and truth came through Jesus Christ.
John 1:17

When Jesus taught the people, He compared the word of God to a seed. When you plant a seed in good soil and water and weed it, it will grow and become strong and have good roots.

It's the same with the word of God. God's word is the seed. The good soil is your heart. When you read the bible, you are planting God's word in your heart. You water it by studying the bible. You weed it by not letting the things of this world come between you and God.

And the cares of this world and the deceitfulness of riches and the lusts of other things entering in choke the word and it becomes unfruitful.
Mark 4:19

The love and patience that you put toward caring for the
seed, reading and hearing God's word, the stronger you
will grow in faith and in knowing God's heart
and the kingdom of heaven.

When you know, believe and trust in God's word,
that seed becomes a mighty tree.

The kingdom of heaven is like a mustard seed, which a man took and sowed in his field, which
indeed is the least of all seeds; but when it is grown it is greater than the herbs and becomes a
tree, so that the birds of the air come and nest in its branches.
Matthew 13: 31-32

So then faith comes by hearing, and hearing by the word of God.
Romans 10:17

God's word is true. His word is a promise that you can depend on. The bible is full of God's promises and lessons for you to learn and live by.

When you follow God's word, life gets much easier.

God's word is powerful!

For the word of God is living and powerful, and sharper than any two-edged sword...
Hebrews 4:12

God's word has taught me that if I am honest and truthful
and treat people with honor, respect and kindness,
that I will have success in everything I do.

This book of law shall not depart from your mouth, but you shall meditate in it day and night,
that you may observe to do according to all that is written in it. For then you will
make your way prosperous and then you will have good success.
Joshua 1:8

Lemonade 5¢
encouraging words FREE
puppy kisses FREE Too!

The bible says we need to put on the whole armor of God and carry the sword of the Spirit, which is the word of God. So Oscar and I went and got our armor from mom's kitchen.

God's word will teach you what Jesus did for us.
It will show you your identity and the authority you have through Christ Jesus.

I have faith. I know the truth. Jesus has made me righteous and has given me my salvation.
I am prepared to tell everyone about the peace of God and I carry God's word in my bible and in me.

I am ready for anything!

Therefore take up the whole armor of God... having girded your waist with truth...
put on the breastplate of righteousness... shod your feet with the preparation of the gospel of peace...
the shield of faith... the helmet of salvation and the sword of the spirit which is the word of God.
Ephesians 6:13-17

If I'm sad or having a bad day, I read and think on God's promises and that gives me peace and joy. I know God's word is true and His promises are always good.

You will keep him in perfect peace, whose mind is stayed on You.
Isaiah 26:3

In your presence is fullness of joy.
Psalm 16:11

So shall My word be that goes forth from My mouth; it shall not return to Me void.
Isaiah 55:11

When you think on God's word it can change the way you feel. But Jesus also taught us that our words are important too. We don't like it when someone says hurtful words to us, so we should always be mindful of the words we choose to speak. You have the ability to change someone's frown into a smile when you give them a kind and encouraging word.

Death and life are in the power of the tongue.
Proverbs 18:21

The heart of the righteous studies how to answer.
Proverbs 15:28

I like to read the stories in the bible to my friends. Oscar likes to hear the stories too. So he invites all of his friends. They especially like the story of Noah's ark.

When you find yourself in a situation and you don't know what to do or which way you should turn; turn to God for the answers. The Holy Spirit will bring back to your remembrance His word and it will always guide you and instruct you.

It's like a light shining on your path, showing you the way.

Hey, there is a scripture that says that!
Thank you Holy Spirit!

Your word is a lamp to my feet, and a light to my path.
Psalm 119:105

Accepting Jesus

To know love is to know Jesus. And to know Jesus is to know God the Father, because God is love. If you want to know Jesus and the Father's love, ask Him into your life. He will show you and tell you all about His love for you, just like He did with me.

Just say;

"Jesus, I believe in my heart you are the Son of God and that you are my Lord and Savior. By faith in Your word I ask you into my life and I receive my salvation now. Thank you Jesus for saving me."

Recieve the Holy Spirit

If you just said that prayer and accepted Jesus into your life, or if Jesus is already part of your life, then God the Father wants to give you His Holy Spirit.

The Holy Spirit will live in you and will guide you and teach you in the way of the Father. All you have to do is ask, believe and receive.

Just say;

"Father, I ask for your power and your guidance to live this new life you have for me. Please fill me with Your Holy Spirit. I recieve Him right now. Thank you for baptizing me with Your Holy Spirit."

www.ingramcontent.com/pod-product-compliance
Lightning Source LLC
Chambersburg PA
CBHW042121040426

42449CB00003B/133